Charles S. Ricketts, Charles Shannon

The Dial

Charles S. Ricketts, Charles Shannon

The Dial

ISBN/EAN: 9783742805034

Manufactured in Europe, USA, Canada, Australia, Japa

Cover: Foto ©Andreas Hilbeck / pixelio.de

Manufactured and distributed by brebook publishing software
(www.brebook.com)

Charles S. Ricketts, Charles Shannon

The Dial

LA VIE ÉLARGIE

En ces villes d'ombre et d'ebène,
Où buissonnent des feux prodigieux,
En ces villes, où se démènent,
Avec leurs pleurs, leurs ruts et leurs blasphèmes,
A grande houle, les foules ;
En ces villes soudain terrifiées
De fête rouge ou de nocturne effroi,
Je sens grandir et s'exalter en moi,
Et fermenter soudain, mon cœur multiplié.

La fièvre, avec de frémissantes mains,
La fièvre, au vent de la folie et de la haine,
M'entraîne
Et me roule, comme un caillou, par les chemins.
Ma volonté s'annule et se supprime,
Mon cœur bondit, soit vers la gloire ou vers le crime,
Et tout-à-coup je m'apparais celui
Qui s'est, hors de soi même, enfui
Vers un irrésistible appel des forces unanimes.

Soit rage ou bien amour ou bien démence,
Tout passe, en vol de foudre, au fond des consciences,
Tout se devine, avant qu'on ait senti
Le clou d'un but profond entrer dans son esprit.
Des gens hagards échevèlent des torches,
Une rumeur de mer s'engouffre au fond des porches ;
Murs, enseignes, maisons, palais, gares,
Dans le soir fou, devant mes yeux, s'effarent ;
Sur les places, des poteaux d'or et de lumière,
Tendent, vers les cieux noirs, des feux qui s'exaspèrent ;
Un cadran luit, couleur de sang, au front des tours ;
Qu'un tribun parle, au coin d'un carrefour,
Avant que l'on comprenne un sens à ses paroles,
Deja l'on suit son geste—et c'est, avec fureur,
Qu'on jette à terre et qu'on outrage un empereur,
Qu'on brise et qu'on abat le socle, où luit l'idole.

La nuit est colossale et géante de bruit,
Une électrique ardeur brule dans l'atmosphère,
Les cœurs sont à prendre ; l'âme se serre
En une une angoisse énorme, et se délivre en cris ;
On sent qu'un seul instant est maître
D'épanouir ou d'écraser ce qui va naitre ;
Le peuple est à celui que le destin
Dota d'assez puissantes mains,
Pour manœuvrer la foudre et les tonnerres,

Et

Et dévoiler parmi tant de lueurs contraires
L'astre nouveau que chaque ère nouvelle
Choisit pour aimanter la vie universelle.

Oh dis, sens tu, qu'elle est belle et profonde,
Mon cœur,
Cette heure,
Qui crie et frappe au cœur du monde?

Que t'importent et les vieilles sagesses,
Et les soleils couchants des dogmes dans la mer ;
Voici l'heure qui bout de sang et de jeunesse,
Voici la formidable et merveilleuse ivresse
D'un vin si fou, que rien n'y semble amer.
Un large espoir, venu de l'Inconnu, déplace
L'équilibre ancien dont les âmes sont lasses ;
La nature parait sculpter
Un visage nouveau à son éternité ;
Tout bouge—et l'on dirait les horizons en marche.
Les ponts, les tours, les arches
Tremblent au fond du sol profond,
La multitude et ses brusques poussées
Semblent faire éclater les villes oppressées,
L'heure a sonné des debâcles et des miracles
Et des gestes d'éclair et d'or,
Là bas au loin, sur les Thabors.

Comme une vague en des vagues fondue,
Comme une aile perdue au fond de l'étendue,
Engouffre toi
Mon cœur, en ces foules, battant les capitales
De leurs terreurs et de leurs rages triomphales.
Vois s'irriter et s'exalter
Chaque clameur, chaque folie et chaque effroi ;
Fais un faisceau de ces milliers de fibres,
Muscles tendus et nerfs qui vibrent ;
Aimante et réunis tout ces courants—et prends
Si large part à ces brusques métamorphoses
D'hommes et choses,
Que tu sentes l'obscure et formidable loi
Qui les domine et les opprime
Soudainement, à coups d'éclairs, se préciser en toi.

Mets en accord ta force avec les destinées
Que la foule, sans le savoir,
Promulgue en cette nuit d'angoisse illuminée.
Ce que sera, demain, le droit de devoir,

2

Seule,

Seule, elle en a l'instinct profond,
Et l'univers total s'attèle et collabore
Avec ses millions de causes qu'on ignore
A chaque effort vers le futur, qu'elle élabore
Rouge et tragique, au fond des horizons.

Oh! l'avenir, comme on l'écoute
Crever le sol, casser les voûtes,
En ces villes d'ébène et d'or, où l'incendie
Rôde, comme un lion dont les crins s'irradient ;
Minute unique, où les siècles tressaillent,
Nœud que les victoires dénouent dans les batailles,
Grande heure, où les aspects du monde changent
Où ce qui fut juste et sacré paraît étrange
Où l'on monte vers les sommets d'une autre foi,
Où la folie, en ses tempêtes,
Forge la vérité nouvelle, et la décrète,
Et l'affranchit de la gâine de lois
Comme un glaive trop grand pour le fourreau
Et trop clair et trop pur pour le bourreau.

En ces villes soudain terrifiées
De fête rouge et de nocturne effroi,
Pour te grandir et te magnifier
Mon âme, enferme toi.

EMILE VERHAEREN.

3

OPEN THE DOOR, POSY!

POSY and her mother lay side by side, quite still and white upon the bed. The air was hot and dry and still, and out of the window of their poor cabin the heat-haze could be seen overhanging the roofs of the town. But Posy and her mother never lifted a finger to disturb themselves as they lay, nor raised an eyelid to look out.

At the end of the bed sat Death, the Taxman, looking at them. Presently he said, " Where is my loaf of bread? How is it you have not got my loaf of bread for me? "

Posy's mother answered, " We were too poor. We were a week without food ourselves; and then came the fever; and then you came."

" That is a common story in these parts just now! " said Death. " But to make an end of this; if you cannot buy me a loaf you must go to the Poor-house to get it."

Then Posy got down off the bed, and went to the door. She felt quite light and thin in the sunshine; and as she walked through the town nothing moved out of her way, or recognised her at all. In the middle of the town she came to the sluggish market-place: there were the booths standing, but few people bought or sold. She wanted to cry, but her tears would no longer go out into the living world, but fell back upon her heart, burning it like fire.

" If I could get some one to give me a loaf here," she said to herself, " I need not go on to the Poor-house." She stopped at the first booth and asked. The woman went on crying her wares. She stopped at the second booth and asked; but the woman only cried her wares. " They cannot see me," she thought; and she stopped at the third booth, and put out her hand.

She reached up on tip-toe: she was very small. " I have asked," she said to herself, " and they have not said no." And she took a loaf.

When she got back she gave the loaf to Death the Taxman, and lay down by her mother again. As he was going, he called back through the doorway, " Mind you be ready for Death the Undertaker when he comes. And if he doesn't come soon you'd better call him."

Posy and her mother lay still on the bed for the rest of that day and all the night. In the morning the mother said, " Get up and look out, Posy; and if you see him, call him in." Posy got up, and looked, and came back again. " I don't see any one, mother, except a pedlar going along the road carrying his pack."

After a little time her mother said, " Look again! " And Posy looked, and came and lay down, saying, " I only saw a man going along carrying a Punch and Judy show on his back."

Then after a time her mother said, " Look again! " and Posy looked and said, " There is a man coming up to the door with a coffin on his back; and it is the same as the pedlar and the Punch and Judy man."

When Death the Undertaker unlatched the door and looked in, he saw the mother and daughter both lying still on the bed, all ready in their

4   shrouds

shrouds. They were so thin he put them both into the same coffin, and seemed hardly to feel their weight as he carried them away. On the road he grumbled to himself because they were paupers and had left no money for him. Presently he threw the coffin down on the ground, and went away leaving it.

In a little while came Death the Sexton; and he, when he saw them, grumbled to his shovel because there was no money left on the coffin to pay him for digging the hole. He dug only a little way and then stopped, slipping the coffin in endways. Then he covered it over with earth which he trampled and beat down with a spud; and at last he too went away.

There was no fireplace, and no window, only a plain door; and the mother and her child lay for a long time side by side, just as they had lain on the bed in their little cabin by the town.

Presently there was a sound outside of a scraping in the earth, and the knock of a hand on the wood. "Get up, and open the door, Posy," said her mother. And Posy went and opened the door.

There was an old man, and with him two old women rubbing the mould from their eyes and looking in to see who was there. "So *you* are here, are you?" said the old man, "you who were always so proud!" "You kept yourself pretty stiff and highty-tighty, Missus; you did that," remarked one of the old women; "but you've committed felony, it seems, and were a pauper, which is worse." "Well, we're neighbours now," added the other woman; "you being in pauper's ground, which is next to the criminals. It isn't any of them proud folk who'll come and look in on you now."

Posy's mother began smoothing down the crinkles of her shroud, as her habit had been with her apron when she was a decent body in the world above. In a little while she would let them know something! Who were these disreputable old neighbours that dared come and speak to her now? She peered round the door to make out what they were like.

"I know you, Daddy Springfeather," she cried at last, "you that was hung for sheep-stealing, to be sure!"

"Not so bad as loaf-stealing!" answered the old man and the two old women.

"And you, and you," went on Posy's mother, pointing at them angrily; "you were the two old rag-pickers who never spent a penny but on drink, and died of that!"

"Better than dying a pauper," answered the two old women.

"Better it isn't: but I'm neither a pauper nor a loaf-stealer!" cried Posy's mother. "And you can get out of my doorway, for my coffin's paid for in the hem of the skirt that hangs up behind the door!"

"This coffin," said the old man feeling it with his thumb, "is no more paid for than it's mahogany: and if you didn't send your daughter to steal a loaf off Mealyman the baker at his booth in the market-place, you go round and ask him; for he's just come down, having been struck on the left cheek by Fever, while he was loving of Famine with his right."

5   "Posy,"

"Posy," said her mother, shutting the door against her assailants, so as to speak with her daughter alone, "what did you do when you went to fetch the bread?"

Then Posy told her mother all about it : and said her mother—"Where were our wits that we forgot to tell Death the Undertaker of the money in the hem of the skirt behind the door ; which we never touched during the famine because it was to be for our funerals? Posy, my child, a pauper's coffin is a thing I can't sleep in! This has got to be set right."

Before long she heard Death the Sexton digging near, for it was paupers' ground, and the deaths were numerous. Then she began to cry —"Death the Sexton, come and take us out! Death the Sexton, come and take us out!"

When Death the Sexton heard that he laughed. "Oh, I daresay!" he said. "And why should that be?"

Said Posy's mother, "Because you have buried us in a pauper's coffin." "And what have you to say against that?" "Only this," said Posy's mother ; "the money for our funeral is in the hem of my skirt that is hanging behind the door ; and unless I'm dug up, and buried again properly, how can you expect to get paid?"

Directly Death the Sexton heard that, about being paid, he came in a great hurry and dug up Posy and her mother and the coffin, and dumped them down outside the burial ground.

Presently Death the Undertaker came by, and Posy's mother began to cry, "Death the Undertaker, come and carry us back to my house! Death the Undertaker, come and carry us back to my house!"

Death the Undertaker stopped, and began laughing. "Why that?" he asked at last. "Because," said Posy's mother, "you have put us into a pauper's coffin, when all the time the money for the coffin is in the hem of my skirt hanging behind the door ; and we want to go back and pay our way from the beginning properly."

Directly Death the Undertaker heard her speak about paying her way, he stopped laughing quickly enough, and took up the coffin and carried it back to the little cabin, and laid Posy and her mother back on to the bed, and went away to get a better coffin.

Presently the mother heard Death the Taxman going by. "Death the Taxman, Death the Taxman!" she cried ; "come and give us back the loaf we stole for you!"

Death the Taxman came in grumbling. "You may well say 'stole' ; I wasn't able to eat it. I never found out till afterwards, or you shouldn't have got buried. What I eat for my wage has to be come by honestly."

"Well," said Posy's mother, "all you have got to do is to let us go, for there's money in the hem of the skirt hanging there behind the door ; and then we can buy you bread that you can eat."

So Death the Taxman let Posy and her mother go. And when they came to life again they found themselves quite well and hearty after their long rest ; and the fever was gone from the town, and the famine was
6   over ;

over; and said Posy's mother, looking round, and beginning to tidy the house, "Since we *are* here again, we had better stop."

But in a short time came Death the Taxman, and Death the Undertaker, and Death the Sexton, all clamoring to be paid and have their victims.

"All in good time," said Posy's mother. "*You* send back Famine and Fever, and set them to catch us; and as soon as ever they've caught us again, depend upon it, we'll come! But until then——My word! what are you Silly Billies standing there for? Shut the door, Posy!"

LAURENCE HOUSMAN.

7

PHANTOM SEA-BIRDS.

Sirs, though ocean's gapless bound
Ever-same do gird us round,
Fix the eye on glowing haze
Which the sun's late-lingering rays
Crimson like anemones
That butterflies in woodland kiss :—
With the East-wind at our back,
Ere the tilting blue turn black,
Though the prow duck to the dips,
And abrupt waves slap the ship's
Bellied bows whose timber thrills,
We may see the poppied hills,
Safe in ward of magic, steer,
Summer-sweet, o'er surges drear,
With the rambling palace, rich
Home of Circe, island-witch,
Daughter of the inisled Sun,
Whom false Persa lured and won,
Long held fast and kissed and kissed,
Having couched her like a mist,
Where the salt, waste, marshy fens
Find sea-monsters brackish dens :
Helios lay there on the rushes
Which the booming storm-wind crushes,
Blushing gorgeously for shame—
Lay for hours all the same.—
Hark, perhaps a Siren sings,
Viewless talons, tail and wings ;
Deadly, deadly now their charm
With no outward show of harm.
Listen, listen, back the ear
With the hollow hand, to hear.

" The air is alive, yet fear no ill ;
Let the helm loose, and trust our skill ;
Free the tugging sail with a jerk,
For we can do all manner of work.
Safe as a bubble on milk new drawn,
Drift like a curled moon before the dawn :—
Dreams that merge in a dream more vast,
Your lives shall merge in life at last,
Where death shall loom no more, but frame the past,
As frames a park an open palace-door,
Where leaves blown in ne'er reach across the floor
To kings whose minds hark back, but their wounds grow
    not sore.

Fear,

Fear, there, seems childish passion, known no longer;
Each sense has leisure; memory, though stronger,
Yet veils what else might tempt the fond heart to deplore.
A queen shall fill the crystal up with wine,
To bathe your lips still smarting from the brine;
And you shall tread,
Bare-foot, on petals shed;
And you shall lie in jasmine-trellised bed,
Dream, meet with any friend alive or dead;
Obedient sleep,
Prolonged for rapture deep,
Shall let each soul her chosen comrade keep
And to the full in boon communion steep.—
Turn once to hear,
True lips will brush your ear,
Our bodies in your arms be real and dear—
One whom you loved in vain, at last, drawn near.

"Woe! woe!
Let honey flow,
Let the sharp blush come and go,
Draw thick drops from the breast's too passive snow!
O talons, let
A warm red rainfall wet
The unmoved faces, dew the stiff beard's jet!
Ere it be vain,
Choke down this sobbing pain!
Sing, with the lips where many found great gain,
The whole of love,
The births and deaths thereof,
Timed to the wings of some spray-drenchèd dove,
Whose pink feet dip
In the long wave's eager lip,
While faintness numb invades each frail plume-tip!—
Love, in our arms
We nurse and lull thy qualms,
Yet never felt or feel thy sovereign charms.
Our hearts are cold;
Love, a new tale, was told -
In our young ears—now has the tale grown old,
Love still unknown,
Whose praise, and that alone,
Has mocked our ears: our hearts are still our own.
Those who praised him,
Knit with us limb in limb,
Died blind with bliss while yet our eyes were dim.

9   Still

Still would we try,
Before our sweetness fly,
With you to capture Love, share Love, and die."

Turn, turn with a welling tear
And a pleasure-cozened ear :—
See, the huge black canvas bars
Half the fully-wakened stars,
While the tackle's tarry smell
Faintly from the hold doth tell.
Ah! the bleak mid-ocean plain,
Sad Persephone's cold field,
Heaves with no rich golden grain,
But salt tears and sleep its yield.—
Queen, now on these furrows rocked,
May our brains from dreams be locked.

T. STURGE MOORE.

THE FATE OF THE CROSSWAYS.

THE roads met and crossed in front of an angle of wayside grass, across which ran the wall of an olive-farm. Along the top of this wall a dozen or more pollard cypresses grew together, the elastic forwardness of their growth restrained by informal wattles. Two cypresses, unstinted in height, stood erect at either end of the dark hedge, with beautiful formality like towers, a little in advance of the others, since the wall made a shallow curve just where they rose. Against the wall, half-way up its grey surface, a stone seat had been built, a seat transformed by weather and use almost to a natural object.

It seemed as if the builders expected that many people would sit down on the long bench at that place; yet as I approached I only saw one figure in the centre—a woman's. Her dress was dark and her thin fingers lay on it at the knee, quite white and without movement of any kind. Her feet had such hold of the ground they seemed to chain it. But the veil round her head was fluttering and milky, her pale eyeballs drew in the light till they were full of its beatitude, and the whole face conveyed to the beholder such activity of an indwelling mind, in spite of the unusual features, that the impression weighed down one's breath. She seemed to be a goddess, to belong to the universe just by the way she sat in that common afternoon glow, beside that bit of wall.

I could not speak to her, and she did not move to look at me, although I felt she drew me into her eyes, as she drew the light. I stood before her, because I had to choose my road, for I was at crossways in my journey. Should I turn to right or left? As I hesitated and cast about, a most singular sense came over me that the seat was crowded. I could see nothing; but as one feels there is teeming life in the grass, or in the stream, when one's perception is sensitive with its own life, so I felt that seat occupied by presences, from the woman's figure in the centre to the cypress towers at each end. And I knew that as I was drawn into the goddess's eyes like the light, so these unseen companions of hers hung on my choice as earthly things hang on the changes of the weather. With a fear that was nearly blind, and intensity that was actual anguish, I made my choice. . . . . I will not say whether to right or left.

But I had not gone far along the road, before all the fierce dogs in the neighbouring farms began to howl in chorus, as if it had been midnight instead of afternoon. I looked back—the woman was gone and the seat was empty with the extreme voidness of a church at mid-day.

Then the truth came to me clear.

I had been in the presence of Hecate—the dogs howled again—of Hecate and the Souls of the Dead who wander with her.

I sank down on my new road—if with adoration or mere collapse I cannot tell.

Ye Fates of the Wheel of Necessity, Clotho, Lachesis and Atropa, ye are nothing as compared with the Fate of the Crossways, Hecate, who wanders with the Dead.

The dogs no longer howled, but whimpered, and I went on direct.

11   MICHAEL FIELD.

SAINT IVES, CORNWALL.

The rock is all a piled and burrowed town,
As though the sea had wrought its balanced shelves
And crannies, wherein men may hide themselves,
Like lobsters in dark nooks, and lie them down.
The slimy-booted rockman, in his brown
Hard vest, glides slipperily as the elves
He hunts ; not loutishly like him who delves ;
The man of prey thus different from the clown.
'Twas he who built this fortress.   Is its shape
His overcraft towards the fish, to ape
The rock the fishes fear not ?   Glideth he
Lest peeping fish should mark him from the sea ?
And when he speaketh, is't with wave-tuned breath
Lest the shy fish should hear him, what he saith ?

JOHN GRAY.

LEDA.

The heavy air hangs faint
And tangled ; so no bird complaint
Athwarts it ; songs of beetles swoon
Upon the heavy afternoon.

Leda, for greed of shade,
And eager faltering through the glade
Of stammering, pleading feet, lets fall
The fetter of her purple pall ;

And, folding her bright hair
Within the twin frail fillet, bare
Lays all the treasure of her neck,
Adorned with one blue jewel fleck

Hung to a tender cord,
The circling crease, which doth afford
Steadfast, exact similitude :
The ring of Venus and her brood.

The gleaming grass lies prone :
The yews seem bronze, the poplars stone.
The very flowers at Leda's feet
Distil a desolating heat.

Refreshing shade is not.
The darkness of the mossy plot
The willows shelter, doth oppress
The air with added heaviness.

All palpitant and dazed,
Across the lawn doth Leda haste,
To where the dreaming water lies ;
Therein to cool her mirrored eyes.

A bubbly fount makes wet
The low contiguous parapet ;
Recumbent in a wealth of green,
Against the same doth Leda lean.

The fountain's splash beyond,
In stiller reaches of the pond,
Where weakest ripples spend their strength,
Despairing to attain its length,

The awful heavens burn
Repeated in the hollows ; yearn
With ruddier purpose, to unfold
The swelling destiny they hold.

And.

And, in a certain place,
Suspended on the water's face,
The doubled swans sit motionless,
For ease against the summer stress.

Yet, lo, why stoop their crests
Contritely to their fluttering breasts,
Which hurrying wavelets break upon?
Hush, Leda, whence this goodly swan,

This new majestic third,
Unmated, as becomes a bird
So proud imperious? (For so fair
A fowl were matchless anywhere.)

Incomparable down
Of breast, and red-billed royal frown,
And gradual wings outspread to fold,
And back most lustrous to behold,

Are but the little part
Of his enticement, which doth start
From jocund curl of every plume,
A stalwart song, a cool perfume.

THE SWAN :
Though grasses deep
Contrive to keep
Whole for memory, and cherish
The print thy form
Leave deep and warm,
Leda, lady, grasses perish.

Essay the pool,
O beautiful
Leda, for a softer cushion ;
Glorious float
About thy throat,
Pillow fair, thy hair's profusion.

Thine arm let deck
My willing neck,
Naught let trouble or afear thee ;
So on the tide
Against his side
Haughtily thy swan shall bear thee

14   Into

Into a nook
Of gorgeous look,
Gay with strange and varied shadow,
Whereof the floor
Is even more
Flowered than the Elysian meadow.

With which the swan floats near ;
And bidding Leda not to fear
Adventure with him, by the beck
Of his keen eyes and writhing neck,

Enticeth till her breast
Beyond the parapet doth rest ;
Until a timid hand leans out
And folds his downy breast about.

Over the margin slips
The lithe blithe line of Leda's hips ;
And straightway hence the swan doth speed,
Exultant for his rapturous deed,

The glory of their course :
Whence his quick gesture and his force
Excite the like in Leda's limbs,
Who, like a sturdy swimmer, swims

Beside her feathered lord,
And swift assistance doth afford.
Athwart where pendant vines above
Curtain a shallow water grove,

The swan and Leda break
Triumphant from the spreading lake ;
And pause beneath acacias' shade,
Which drops perfume, a sheer cascade.

Till sudden lightnings split
The burning sky, and empty it ;
And raucously as eagles cry
An eagle screamed across the sky.

JOHN GRAY.

15

THE CENTAUR.
(FROM THE FRENCH OF MAURICE DE GUÉRIN.)

T was given me to be born in the caves of these mountains. As with the river of this valley, whose first drops flow from some rock weeping in a deep recess, the earliest moments of my life fell upon the gloom of a secluded abode, and that without disturbing its silence. When the mothers of our race feel themselves about to be delivered, they keep apart, and near the caverns; then, in the most forbidding depths, in the thickest of the darkness, they bear, without a cry, offspring as silent as themselves. Their mighty milk enables us to surmount the early straits of life without languor or doubtful struggle; nevertheless we leave our caverns later than you your cradles. For it is generally received among us, that one should withhold and everyway shield existence at the outset, counting those days to be engrossed by the gods. My growing-up ran almost its entire course in that darkness wherein I was born. Our abode at its innermost lay so far within the thickness of the mountain, that I should not have known on which side there might be an issue, if, turning astray through the entrance, the winds had not sometimes driven in thither freshets of air and sudden commotions. Also, at times, my mother returned, having about her the perfume of valleys, or streaming from waters which she frequented. These home-comings, which she made without ever instructing me about glens or rivers, but followed by their emanations, disquieted my spirit, so that, much agitated, I roamed the darkness. "What are they," I said to myself, "these *withouts* whither my mother betakes herself, and what is it that reigns there of such power as to call her to itself so frequently? But what can that be, which is experienced there, of nature so contrarious, that she returns every day diversely moved?" My mother came home, now animated by a deep-seated joy, then again sad, trailing her limbs, and as it were wounded. The joy which she brought back announced itself from afar in certain features of her walk and was shed abroad in her glances. It was communicated throughout my whole being; but her prostration gained on me even more and drew me much farther along those conjectures into which my spirit would go forth. At such moments I was perturbed on account of my own powers, and used to recognise therein a principle that could not dwell alone; then betaking myself either to whirl my arms about, or to redouble my galloping in the spacious darkness of the cavern, I spurred myself on to discover, by the blows which I struck in the void and the rush of the pace I made, that toward which my arms were intended to reach out and my feet to carry me... Since then I have knotted my arms about the bust of centaurs, and the bodies of heroes, and the trunks of oaks; my hands have gained experience of rocks, of waters, of the innumerable plants, and of subtilest impressions from the air: for I lift them up, on blind calm nights, in order that they may take knowledge of any passing breaths and draw from thence signs of augury to determine my path. For my feet, behold, O Melampus! how they are worn away! And nevertheless, all

16   numbed

numbed as I am—subject to the extremities of old age, there are days whereon, in broad daylight upon the hilltops, I start off on those racings of my youth in the caverns—to the same end brandishing my arms and putting forth all that remains of my fleetness.

Those fits of turbulence would alternate with long periods of cessation from all unquiet movement. Straightway, throughout my entire being, I no longer possessed any other sensation save that of growth, and of the gradual progress of life as it mounted within my breast. No more caring to career about, recoiled upon an absolute repose, I used to savour in its integrity the good effected by the gods while it worked through me. Calm and darkness preside over the secret charm of conscious life. Ye glooms, which dwell in caverns of these mountains, to your tendance I owe the underlying education that has so powerfully fostered me, and this, also, that in your keeping I tasted life wholly pure, such as it flows at first, welling from among the gods. When I descended from your fastnesses into the light of day, I staggered and saluted it not. For it laid hold on me with violence, making me drunk as some malignant liquor might have done, suddenly poured through my veins; and I felt that my being, till then so compact and simple, underwent shaking and loss, as though it had been destined to disperse upon the winds.

O Melampus, by what design of the gods have you, who desire knowledge of the life led by centaurs, been guided to me, the oldest and saddest of them all? It is now a long while that I have ceased from all active share in their life. I no longer leave the heights of this mountain whereon age has confined me. The point of my arrows serves now only to root up tenacious plants. Tranquil lakes know me still, but the rivers have forgotten me. To you I will impart certain things concerning my youth; but such memories, issuing from a dried-up source, lag like the streams of a niggard libation, falling from a damaged urn. I easily pictured for you my earliest years, because they were calm and perfect; simple life, and that only, slaked all craving. Such things are both retained in the mind and recounted without difficulty. If a god were besought to narrate his life, it would be done in two words, O Melampus.

My youth was of wont hurried and full of agitation. I lived for movement and knew no limit to my going. In the pride of my unfettered powers, I wandered about, visiting all parts of these wildernesses. One day as I was following a valley little frequented by centaurs, I came upon a man making his way along by the river, on its opposite bank. He was the first my eyes had chanced upon; I despised him. "There at most," said I, "is but the half of me! How short his steps are, and how uneasy his gait! His eyes seem to measure space with sadness. Doubtless it is some centaur, degraded by the gods, one whom they have reduced to dragging himself along like that."

Often, for relaxation after the day, I would seek some river bed. One half of me, beneath the surface, was exerted to keep me up, while the other raised itself tranquilly, and I carried my arms idly, out of reach of the waves; becoming oblivious thus in the midst of the waters, and

17   yielding

yielding to the sweep of their course, which would bear me far away, and escort their wild guest past every charm of their banks. How many times, overtaken by night, have I not followed the stream under the spreading darkness, that let fall, even to the depths of the valleys, the nocturnal influence of the gods! Then my headlong life would become tempered till there was left but a faint sense of existence, equably apportioned throughout my whole being; even as throughout the waters in which I was swimming, there was a glimmer infused, shed by that goddess who traverses the night. Melampus, my old age yearns after the rivers; peaceful and monotonous for the most part, they take their appointed way with more calm than centaurs, and with a wisdom more beneficent than that of men. On coming up out of them I was followed by their bounties, which would continue with me for whole days, and take long in dispersing, after the manner of perfumes.

My steps used to be at the disposal of a wild and blind waywardness. In the midst of the most violent racings it would happen that my gallop was suddenly broken off, as though my feet had stopped short of an abyss, or as though a god stood upright before me. Such sudden immobility would allow me to savour my life thrilled through in the very heat of a present access. In those days, too, I have cut branches in the forest, that, while running, I have held above my head; the swiftness of my motion would suspend the restlessness of the foliage, which no longer caused any but the faintest rustle; but on the least pause, the wind and tumult re-entered the bough, which again resumed the volume of its wonted murmur. Thus my life, on the sudden interruption of the impetuous rush that I could command across these valleys, quivered throughout me. I used to hear it course, all boiling, as it drove on the internal fire which had been kindled by passage through space so ardently traversed. My flanks, exhilarated, opposed the tides by which they were crushed from within, and savoured, during such storms, that luxury, only known else to the shores of the sea, of shutting in, without chance of escape, a life raised to acme pitch and goaded still. Meanwhile, with head inclined to the breeze, which brought me a cool freshness, I contemplated the summits of mountains, distant since a few minutes only—I considered too the trees on the banks and the waters in the rivers, these borne on by a lagging flow, those fastened into the bosom of the earth and only so far endowed with movement as their branches are submissive to the breath of air that compels them to sigh. "Mine only," I said, "is free motion; at will, I transport my life from one end of these valleys to the other. I am happier than torrents that descend mountains never to re-ascend. The sound of my going is more beautiful than the sighing of woods, or than the noise of waters, and, with a voice as of thunder, bespeaks the wandering centaur, who is his own guide." Thus, while my flanks were still possessed by the intoxication of the race, higher up I indulged its pride and, turning my head, remained so for some time, in contemplation of my smoking crupper.

Similar to green and leafy forests teased by winds, Youth heaves to
every

every side with the rich dower of life, and some profound murmur continuously prevails throughout its foliage. Abandoning myself to existence as rivers do, ceaselessly inhaling the effluence of Cybele, were it in the lap of valleys or upon the summit of the mountains, I bounded along every-whither, a mere life, blind and at large. But when the night, replete with the calm of the gods, found me upon the mountain slopes, she constrained me to seek the threshold of some cavern, and soothed me there as she soothes the billows of the sea, permitting survival of such gentle undulations as kept sleep aloof, without however flawing the perfection of repose. Couched on the threshold of my retreat, with flanks hidden in its lair and head under the sky, I followed the pageant of the dark hours with my eyes. Then it was that the foreign life, which interpenetrated me during the day, detached itself little by little, returning to the peaceful bosom of Cybele, as, after the downpour, fragments of rain, caught in the foliage, fall, they too, and rejoin the runnels. It is said that the gods of the sea, during the night-watches, quit their palaces in the deep, and, seating themselves on the promontories, gaze out over the waves. Thus did I keep watch, having at my feet a live expanse resembling a sea drowsed to torpor. Rendered back to full and clear consciousness, it would seem to me as though I came forth from a womb, and that the deep waters, which had conceived me, were but just returned from depositing me upon the height of the mountain, even as a dolphin is left stranded on quicksands by the waves of Amphitrite Goddess of the Shore.

My gaze roved freely and pierced to immense distances. Like an ever humid sea-beach, the range of mountains in the west retained traces of a glory but ill expunged by the darkness. Out there in the wan clearness, persisted, live yet, peaks naked and pure. There I used to watch coming down, now the god Pan, habitually solitary ; now a choir of occult divinities ; or else a mountain nymph would pass, intoxicated by the night. Sometimes the eagles of Mount Olympus traversed the highest heaven and melted away among remote constellations, or vanished, dipping under the inspired woods. The potency of the gods, suddenly rousing into activity, troubled the calm of the old oaks.

You pursue wisdom, O Melampus, wisdom which is science concerning the will of the gods ; and you wander among the nations like a mortal turned from his true path by the destinies. There is hereabouts a stone which, so soon as it is touched, gives forth a sound like to that of the snapping chord of an instrument, and men tell how Apollo, having set down his lyre on this stone, left therein that melodious cry. O Melampus, the wandering gods have rested their lyres upon stones, but none—none has ever forgotten his there. Of old, when I used to keep the night-watches in the caverns, I have sometimes believed that I was about to overhear the dreams of sleeping Cybele, and that the mother of the gods, betrayed by a vision, would let secrets escape her; but I have never made out more than sounds which dissolved in the breath of night, or words inarticulate as the bubbling hum of rivers.

19   "O Macareus,"

"O Macareus," said to me one day the great Chiron, whom I was accustomed to follow in his old age, "both of us are mountain-bred centaurs, but how diverse are we in our habits! As you see, all the solicitude of my days is spent upon research among plants, but you resemble those mortals who have picked up on the waters or in the woods, and carried to their lips, fragments of some reed-pipe broken by god Pan; thenceforth those mortals, having inhaled from such relics of the god a zest for wild life, or being seized on by some occult frenzy, enter the wilderness, plunge into forests, keep company with running waters, or become involved among the mountains, restless, and carried forward on some unconscious enterprise. Mares, paramours of the wind in farthest Scythia, are not wilder than you, nor more downcast at nightfall, when Aquilo has withdrawn himself. Search you after the gods, O Macareus, inquisitive as to whence men are derived, animals and the mainsprings of universal fire? But the old Ocean, father of all things, keepeth these secrets to himself, and, chanting, the nymphs ring him round in an eternal choir, that they may drown whatever might else escape from his lips parted in slumber. Mortals, who by reason of virtue draw nigh to the gods, have received from their hands lyres wherewith to charm nations, or the seeds of new plants wherewith to enrich them; but from their inexorable lips, nothing.

"In my youth Apollo inclined my heart towards the plants, and taught me how to despoil their veins of cordial juices. Since then I have remained faithful to these mountains, my grand abode, restless, but turning with ever renewed application to the quest for simples, and to making known the virtues that I discover. Do you see yonder the bald crown of Mount Oeta? Alcides stripped it in order to construct his pyre. O Macareus! that heroes, children of the gods, should spread out the spoil of lions upon their pyres, and burn themselves to death upon the mountain tops! that the infections of earth should so ravage blood derived from the immortals! And we, centaurs, begotten by an insolent mortal in the womb of a cloud which had the semblance of a goddess, what help should we look for from Jupiter, whose thunderbolt struck down the father of our race? By the god's decree a vulture eternally tears at the entrails of him who fashioned the first man. O Macareus! men and centaurs alike recognise, in the authors of their race, subtractors from the privileges of immortals, apart from whom, perhaps, all that moves is only a petty theft—mere dust of their essence, borne abroad, like seed that floats in the air, by the almighty current of destiny. It is noised about, that Ægeus, father of Theseus, hid, under the weight of a boulder by the sea-side, remembrances and tokens by which his son might, on a future day, recognise his parentage. Somewhere the jealous gods have buried the evidences of universal descent; but by the shore of what sea have they rolled to the stone that covers them, O Macareus?"

Such was the wisdom toward which the great Chiron inclined my heart. Brought down to the extreme verge of old age, that centaur used still to foster in his spirit the loftiest discourse. His bust, vigorous yet, had but
little

little settled back upon his flanks, slightly inclined o'er which, it rose like an oak saddened by the winds ; and the firmness of his step had scarcely been shaken in the course of years. One might have said that he still kept some remnants of the immortality received by him in time past from Apollo, but which he had delivered back to the god.

As for me, O Melampus, I decline into old age calmly, as do the setting constellations. Though I preserve vigour enough to enable me to gain the summit of the crags, whereon I belate myself at nightfall, be it to consider the restless and inconstant clouds, be it to watch mounting up from the horizon the rainy Hyades, the Pleiades or the giant Orion ; none the less I perceive that I dwindle away and suffer loss rapidly, even as a clot of snow floating on a stream, and that in a little I shall make hence, to be mingled with the rivers that take their way across the vast bosom of the earth.

T. Sturge Moore.

OUTAMARO.

IF the art of Japan has made no lasting impression upon England as to its real significance, in France a similar error has been averted by the effort of a few artists and men of letters. It is to them we owe the discovery of Japan. I do not refer here to French imitations of Japanese conventions in the decorative arts, or to mannerisms often common enough to prove that vulgarity is possible even in a country with a "live" tradition, as was the case with Japan some thirty years ago. Efforts have been made abroad that must not be overlooked to understand and class the achievements of Japanese art. If, at the present, there are serious gaps in our knowledge, if much that passes to-day will be set aside to-morrow, modern research has at least brought us thus far. It is now more than thirty years since some coloured prints, rich and strange in tone, excited the attention of a few—among them Edmond de Goncourt. We owe to him the picture of Outamaro in a monograph that places all subsequent admirers in the writer's debt, and from which only generalities and minor inaccuracies may be removed by subsequent research, leaving to him, nevertheless, the first shadowing forth of an artistic personality that is at once definite and elusive, limited yet suggestive, troublesome to the dunce and pedant as the art of Watteau is troublesome.

The qualities of Outamaro have stood the test of various manners of approach, and the exercise of that peculiar gift of fascination that is his, has forced itself upon the attention even of those who had entered upon the study of Japan under the spell of its later magnificent realism. The art of Outamaro will win one also from reactionary mood, due to an over familiarity with the excellent, in a country like Italy, that has had its specious primitives and decadents. We would place Outamaro in a phase of art at once attractive and dangerous, in a phase where, as with Botticelli, an art has refined strangely upon itself, accepting, however, certain signs of fatigue, not, as with the Italian, in technique as from callousness or haste even, but in a tendency towards monotonous trains of thought. In Europe the art of Schöngauer with its over-sweetness, of Zasinger with its delicacy, would hardly prepare one for the might and passion of a Durer, whose art was influenced by them. So the art of Outamaro does not prepare one for the advent of a Hokusai. It is there that he will seem at once primitive and decadent, but, like Botticelli or Memling, Outamaro escapes at times into charmed spaces, and divines, intermittently perhaps, much that those who came before or after him did not divine, or were unable to achieve. A feeling that with this Japanese a monotonous and even feminine bent of mind mars an infinite refinement in form and colour may lead men of intelligence to suspect him, and with him the eighteenth-century art of Japan.

I take it that a certain impatience is manifest among serious art-lovers towards the trade-primitives of Italy, whose hold upon men of the last generation was excusable in the light of discovery and surprise. I do not think, however, that the bankruptcy in the delicate tradition of eighteenth-

century

century art of Japan is entirely comparable to that notable break in the great Tuscan school after the death of Piero della Francesca, a Tuscan by temper. In Japan in the eighteenth century the technical side was developed; we may add that this technical refinement became subsequently a burden. The impeachment of Italy implies a technical collapse. The mind passes from Piero della Francesca to Leonardo for a continuity in restraint and technical perfection. The great violent art of Mantegna and Luca Signorelli seems contemporary with that of Paolo Uccello, and to contain efforts and experiments that Donatello had solved successfully. In Japan, one of the three centres whose tradition may be viewed in its entirety, the art-lover who is never angry or prone to reactionary moods, will accept this phase in which the love of women has absorbed all other attention, and will accept it for what it is.

The mere accidents of a tradition would make of Outamaro an early master of the modern school, "the school of life," and a pioneer in revolt against the conventions of older academies, in a revolution that may be said to culminate in the works of the great Hokusai. This definition, if commonly accepted, is to some extent inaccurate. I would urge that his unique prominence in an epoch of change has numbered him among the quite realistic masters. To aims of his own he added some interests common to the realistic schools, but did they not borrow from him in their earlier works? The spirit in which Outamaro painted has affinities with aristocratic and æsthetic conditions of the Tosa school, whose importance in Japanese art has been too constantly overlooked. I think he shows this mental bent more than his immediate forerunners or older contemporaries in the eighteenth century, with whom the realistic movement is latent, though their manner, like that of Outamaro, has no affinity with Chinese methods; and out of these grew the realistic school.

By the excursions of an exquisite fancy he extended or transformed the subject-matter of his forebears, who treated by preference scenes in the every-day life of ordinary people: scenes noticed by the aristocratic Tosas only in the background of a Court procession. As with the earlier eighteenth-century masters, he retained the Tosa convention of a chastened outline, a recollection of their aristocratic interiors, and the care for dress; something also of their over-wrought languor. The affinities of the Tosa school do not lean towards China. In method the Tosas were an offshoot of those miniaturists come from India with the Buddhist religion. We will find traces of Indian formulæ, in time transformed, it is true, but opposed to the more calligraphic influences of China, that were to be revived by Hokusai, and, at this moment, one is seized with a sense of hallucination; the half-revealed whiteness of an apparition passes across one's eyes beyond the perspective of sanctuaries, as we remember that touch of Hellenic sweetness at the heart of Indian Buddhism, carried with it into the farthest East among a new people and new conditions, not dead at all, but altered, and putting a trace of some remote European manner into this later phase of Japanese art in this eighteenth century.

23   Whatever

Whatever may be the influences upon the work of Outamaro, his colour-harmonies fulfil his own needs and the exigences of the colour print; to the subject-matter of his immediate forerunners he has brought a gift of analysis, an element of the strange, the exquisite, that mere nothing making for grace. His name conjures up the vision of cloud-like colours, and shapes that have the curve of fountains, upon a world remote yet actual, as it would seem to us, for its newness and for its trivialities even, he has shed that grace as of faded things, the troubled hues of a fresco about to disappear, of a flower dying in the twilight.

With Outamaro the attention given to an act, a movement all bright, all gay, all trivial, has acquired by the subtleties of his art a tint of seriousness, of sadness, that never leaves him, that will class him among poetic painters, painters of fancy and of mood. Unlike Hokusai, we are told that dramatic effect lay beyond his aim. He was proud of his achievement as the mere painter of the spring, the painter, the portrait-painter of fair women. At home he was sometimes despised as the artist for the tea-houses, a minister to those frivolous needs of women to whom he brought the new things of fashion and the ways in dress, as a talent full of charm but devoid of all seriousness. Tragic episodes treated by some notion of his, as if acknowledging his limitation, have been given over to women instead of to men, where a haunting sense culminates in the dramatic opposition of an unique black dress to the folds of fairer dresses; or, perhaps, the anxiety faintly shadowed forth about the hour and place by the presence of a naked sword, the implied presence of an end beyond the motions of his actresses. A twist of mind breaks through the constant preoccupation to charm, sometimes the urging of inverted energies pushes him to the erotic and the terrible, but even here he will use majestic lines and chosen colours; we may well marvel at a train of thought so strange to the more downright ways of Europe. Yet we may be mistaken to wonder overmuch. An artist always grasps at hints, giving variety to the aspects of his work, in indifference to the probable effect upon those who would have praised his limitations without effort, or with hostility; such moods of delicate falsity remain not too distinct to the artist himself, for in the exercise of the imaginative faculties thoughts will take motion curiously, as it were from freshets of strange winds, blown from quarters remote; he will feel the countershock of distant events, and there is danger from without in the censure of such "digressions"; they will be found not to answer to the cravings of the affectation or imposture, but to the requirements in the health of an exceptional state. With Outamaro, whose mind was without anxiety or trouble, something of shadow may become noticeable, for half the passions of life and the terribleness of things make their appeal through the eyes to the mind. Let me repeat: his nature leant out towards the fairer aspects of life; it was untroubled by choice, by any emotion outside a world that lived very close to the flowers, in an immunity from anxiety and under conditions we can hardly imagine now and here; yet we have the evidence of other emotions forcing themselves upon him, and he has enriched his work with a passing allusion to them.

24   He

He died having loved too well. He was a great lover of women, whence curious intuitions—feminine intuitions—often present in men of his stamp—expressed here almost for the first time. Natures like his are not averse to the sight of maternity, and in his rendering of women ministering to the little wants of their children he retains a charm denied to the more grave Italian painters of the Madonna. His printed works are numerous. During his lifetime he enjoyed a great reputation that penetrated even to China, and leaf after leaf reveals his quest of the unexpected, directed by a preoccupation for delicate *nuances*—I can find no other word, and not for the sensational element therein. He will select from the fleeting graces of a game, or from the motions of reverie alike. This he clothes with the tints of early anemones and of faded leaves, with tender grey retaining an inward glow or flush, as of colours absorbed by time; his mere paper will be mottled with traces of colour that has been removed, or glazed with a frosted substance like the dried white of an egg. He possesses to the full the resources of a colourist who is always sensitive in the matter of surfaces—the colourist of a country that has several names for white. A common characteristic in his work is the love of mirrors, and of reflections in water used to repeat or introduce an element of interest. In composition he will affect the half-drowned appearance of things bathed in water, as in the two magnificent triptych prints, *Les Plongeuses* and *Les Porteuses de Sel*, veiling the limbs of his women in the twilight of a wave. It serves his purpose to reduce what might be too definite for him, by means of spangled and translucent materials become playthings in the hands of women, as in one of those magnificent prints where a courtesan passes a veil across her mouth and eyes, or in that design charming with its yellows and greens (now in the Louvre), in which a mother peeps at a child from behind a scarf. With him the green haze of mosquito-nets is used for the shadowing forth, beyond, of the half-hidden whiteness of a face, or to make emerge from the shadow a hand or arm with the effect of some flower rising from the water.

If as a colourist he works in a key that rests in a quietude of tones unusual in the art of Europe, we may add to this that time and use have made amort the stronger oppositions of blacks and yellows, or the vivid crossings of white used to freshen any languor of effect, and have given a quality that cannot be found in new surfaces, wearing the crispness of the size out of the paper, making his means more elusive and his colour more grave.

There is often a great attractiveness about things once bright, meant from the first to be captivating when thus greyed by the handling of time ; for this reason men have been found who, like Baudelaire, divined the charm even in old-fashion plates, apart from any sententious interest to be drawn from them, as with our own Thackeray, who wore spectacles. The art of Tanagra passes as a fortunate addition to our enjoyment, brought about by things originally of slight importance, but found now to be exquisite indeed. For the moment the prints of Outamaro do not share this suffrage, in England they are known as yet to the few merely as
25   things

things of curiosity. That I have dwelt upon the slightness of their aims may seem against their being treated too seriously; but art in Japan dwells close to every movement in life, a ministrant jealous of all possible exactness, yet without fear of the indifference of persons like ourselves, jaded to all but novelty, whose appreciation is only one of sudden exclamations, and who ask art to be something added to life, like opium perhaps. The cultured of his country are light of heart, they dismiss the over-positive and the vague alike, but gracefully for what it is; a glint of light, a waif of perfume, the all-absorbing, the gluttonous melancholy at the heart of the East, touches them but little; they are apt to be ironical about it, to pass it by in a verse or a simile with a gaiety that is foreign to us also, at any rate recognising it nobly, as the passion for the few. One of their greatest artists, Outamaro, has accepted these conditions, ministering exquisitely to the needs of an audience that to him was never dull and rarely tired. A great sense of perfection alone reveals that finer sadness from which all sense of perfection is seldom entirely free.

Among slight things of grace few will be found to equal the grace, the charm that is his; his deftness of hand is no mere slightness of execution; and if in this matter it is a little languid beside the more direct brush-work of some Greek vase painters (at times strangely akin to Japanese workers with the brush), his sense of grace will be found to contain also a latent spark of strength almost wholly denied to the sweet popular figurettes of Tanagra; his conventions retain a franker, swifter sense of truth, for which reason he is sometimes classed as a realist; he also meant no more than to *please*, but to please a people whose possibilities for the future had not ceased, and, with all his self-consciousness of means, however complex, he represents the subtlety, the complexity of a tradition that is young, and for this reason his results will remain unforeseen and fresh to us.

CHARLES STURT.

THE DIAL FOR MDCCCXCVII

CONTENTS

THE WRAPPER AND INITIAL LETTERPIECES IN THE TEXT
HAVE BEEN DESIGNED AND ENGRAVED ON THE WOOD BY
CHARLES RICKETTS. THE TWO FULL PAGE PEN DESIGNS
MARKED ABOVE WITH A DEVICE HAVE BEEN REPRODUCED
BY MESSRS. MENTSCHEL AND BY THE SWAN ELECTRIC
ENGRAVING COMPANY. THE LITHOGRAPHS HAVE BEEN
PRINTED BY MR. THOMAS WAY.

.